CELEBRATING
THE MARRIAGE OF

AND

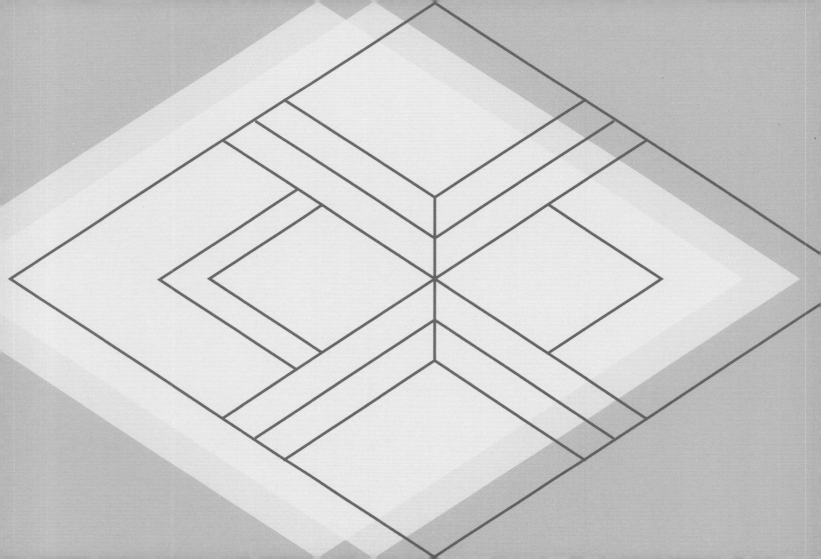

DATE	FROM	EVENT/OCCASION	GIFT/GESTURE	THANK-YOU NOTE FINISHED	DATE SENT
				☐	
				☐	
				☐	
				☐	
				☐	
				☐	
				☐	
				☐	
				☐	

DATE	FROM	EVENT/OCCASION	GIFT/GESTURE	THANK-YOU NOTE FINISHED	DATE SENT
				☐	
				☐	
				☐	
				☐	
				☐	
				☐	
				☐	
				☐	
				☐	

DATE	FROM	EVENT/OCCASION	GIFT/GESTURE	THANK-YOU NOTE FINISHED	DATE SENT

DATE	FROM	EVENT/OCCASION	GIFT/GESTURE	THANK-YOU NOTE FINISHED	DATE SENT
				☐	
				☐	
				☐	
				☐	
				☐	
				☐	
				☐	
				☐	
				☐	

DATE	FROM	EVENT/OCCASION	GIFT/GESTURE	THANK-YOU NOTE FINISHED	DATE SENT
				☐	
				☐	
				☐	
				☐	
				☐	
				☐	
				☐	
				☐	
				☐	

DATE	FROM	EVENT/OCCASION	GIFT/GESTURE	THANK-YOU NOTE FINISHED	DATE SENT
				☐	
				☐	
				☐	
				☐	
				☐	
				☐	
				☐	
				☐	
				☐	

DATE	FROM	EVENT/OCCASION	GIFT/GESTURE	THANK-YOU NOTE FINISHED	DATE SENT
				☐	
				☐	
				☐	
				☐	
				☐	
				☐	
				☐	
				☐	
				☐	

DATE	FROM	EVENT/OCCASION	GIFT/GESTURE	THANK-YOU NOTE FINISHED	DATE SENT
				☐	
				☐	
				☐	
				☐	
				☐	
				☐	
				☐	
				☐	
				☐	

DATE	FROM	EVENT/OCCASION	GIFT/GESTURE	THANK-YOU NOTE FINISHED	DATE SENT
				☐	
				☐	
				☐	
				☐	
				☐	
				☐	
				☐	
				☐	
				☐	

DATE	FROM	EVENT/OCCASION	GIFT/GESTURE	THANK-YOU NOTE FINISHED	DATE SENT
				☐	
				☐	
				☐	
				☐	
				☐	
				☐	
				☐	
				☐	
				☐	

DATE	FROM	EVENT/OCCASION	GIFT/GESTURE	THANK-YOU NOTE FINISHED	DATE SENT
				☐	
				☐	
				☐	
				☐	
				☐	
				☐	
				☐	
				☐	
				☐	

DATE	FROM	EVENT/OCCASION	GIFT/GESTURE	THANK-YOU NOTE FINISHED	DATE SENT
				⌐¬	
				⌐¬	
				⌐¬	
				⌐¬	
				⌐¬	
				⌐¬	
				⌐¬	
				⌐¬	
				⌐¬	

DATE	FROM	EVENT/OCCASION	GIFT/GESTURE	THANK-YOU NOTE FINISHED	DATE SENT
				☐	
				☐	
				☐	
				☐	
				☐	
				☐	
				☐	
				☐	
				☐	

DATE	FROM	EVENT/OCCASION	GIFT/GESTURE	THANK-YOU NOTE FINISHED	DATE SENT
				☐	
				☐	
				☐	
				☐	
				☐	
				☐	
				☐	
				☐	
				☐	

DATE	FROM	EVENT/OCCASION	GIFT/GESTURE	THANK-YOU NOTE FINISHED	DATE SENT
				☐	
				☐	
				☐	
				☐	
				☐	
				☐	
				☐	
				☐	
				☐	

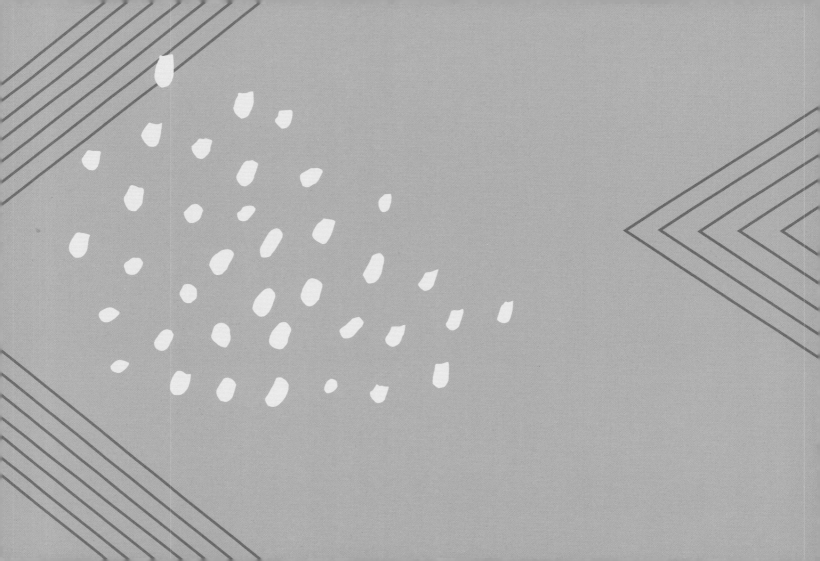

DATE	FROM	EVENT/OCCASION	GIFT/GESTURE	THANK-YOU NOTE FINISHED	DATE SENT
				☐	
				☐	
				☐	
				☐	
				☐	
				☐	
				☐	
				☐	
				☐	

DATE	FROM	EVENT/OCCASION	GIFT/GESTURE	THANK-YOU NOTE FINISHED	DATE SENT
				⌞ ⌟	
				⌞ ⌟	
				⌞ ⌟	
				⌞ ⌟	
				⌞ ⌟	
				⌞ ⌟	
				⌞ ⌟	
				⌞ ⌟	
				⌞ ⌟	

DATE	FROM	EVENT/OCCASION	GIFT/GESTURE	THANK-YOU NOTE FINISHED	DATE SENT
				☐	
				☐	
				☐	
				☐	
				☐	
				☐	
				☐	
				☐	
				☐	

DATE	FROM	EVENT/OCCASION	GIFT/GESTURE	THANK-YOU NOTE FINISHED	DATE SENT
				⬜	
				⬜	
				⬜	
				⬜	
				⬜	
				⬜	
				⬜	
				⬜	
				⬜	

DATE	FROM	EVENT/OCCASION	GIFT/GESTURE	THANK-YOU NOTE FINISHED	DATE SENT
				☐	
				☐	
				☐	
				☐	
				☐	
				☐	
				☐	
				☐	
				☐	

DATE	FROM	EVENT/OCCASION	GIFT/GESTURE	THANK-YOU NOTE FINISHED	DATE SENT
				☐	
				☐	
				☐	
				☐	
				☐	
				☐	
				☐	
				☐	
				☐	

DATE	FROM	EVENT/OCCASION	GIFT/GESTURE	THANK-YOU NOTE FINISHED	DATE SENT
				☐	
				☐	
				☐	
				☐	
				☐	
				☐	
				☐	
				☐	
				☐	

DATE	FROM	EVENT/OCCASION	GIFT/GESTURE	THANK-YOU NOTE FINISHED	DATE SENT
				☐	
				☐	
				☐	
				☐	
				☐	
				☐	
				☐	
				☐	
				☐	

DATE	FROM	EVENT/OCCASION	GIFT/GESTURE	THANK-YOU NOTE FINISHED	DATE SENT

DATE	FROM	EVENT/OCCASION	GIFT/GESTURE	THANK-YOU NOTE FINISHED	DATE SENT
				☐	
				☐	
				☐	
				☐	
				☐	
				☐	
				☐	
				☐	
				☐	

DATE	FROM	EVENT/OCCASION	GIFT/GESTURE	THANK-YOU NOTE FINISHED	DATE SENT
				☐	
				☐	
				☐	
				☐	
				☐	
				☐	
				☐	
				☐	
				☐	

DATE	FROM	EVENT/OCCASION	GIFT/GESTURE	THANK-YOU NOTE FINISHED	DATE SENT
				☐	
				☐	
				☐	
				☐	
				☐	
				☐	
				☐	
				☐	
				☐	

DATE	FROM	EVENT/OCCASION	GIFT/GESTURE	THANK-YOU NOTE FINISHED	DATE SENT
				⌐¬	
				⌐¬	
				⌐¬	
				⌐¬	
				⌐¬	
				⌐¬	
				⌐¬	
				⌐¬	
				⌐¬	

DATE	FROM	EVENT/OCCASION	GIFT/GESTURE	THANK-YOU NOTE FINISHED	DATE SENT
				☐	
				☐	
				☐	
				☐	
				☐	
				☐	
				☐	
				☐	
				☐	

DATE	FROM	EVENT/OCCASION	GIFT/GESTURE	THANK-YOU NOTE FINISHED	DATE SENT
				⌐⌐	
				⌐⌐	
				⌐⌐	
				⌐⌐	
				⌐⌐	
				⌐⌐	
				⌐⌐	
				⌐⌐	
				⌐⌐	

DATE	FROM	EVENT/OCCASION	GIFT/GESTURE	THANK-YOU NOTE FINISHED	DATE SENT
				☐	
				☐	
				☐	
				☐	
				☐	
				☐	
				☐	
				☐	
				☐	

DATE	FROM	EVENT/OCCASION	GIFT/GESTURE	THANK-YOU NOTE FINISHED	DATE SENT
				☐	
				☐	
				☐	
				☐	
				☐	
				☐	
				☐	
				☐	
				☐	

DATE	FROM	EVENT/OCCASION	GIFT/GESTURE	THANK-YOU NOTE FINISHED	DATE SENT
				☐	
				☐	
				☐	
				☐	
				☐	
				☐	
				☐	
				☐	

DATE	FROM	EVENT/OCCASION	GIFT/GESTURE	THANK-YOU NOTE FINISHED	DATE SENT
				⌞ ⌝	
				⌞ ⌝	
				⌞ ⌝	
				⌞ ⌝	
				⌞ ⌝	
				⌞ ⌝	
				⌞ ⌝	
				⌞ ⌝	
				⌞ ⌝	

DATE	FROM	EVENT/OCCASION	GIFT/GESTURE	THANK-YOU NOTE FINISHED	DATE SENT
				☐	
				☐	
				☐	
				☐	
				☐	
				☐	
				☐	
				☐	
				☐	

DATE	FROM	EVENT/OCCASION	GIFT/GESTURE	THANK-YOU NOTE FINISHED	DATE SENT
				⌐⌐	
				⌐⌐	
				⌐⌐	
				⌐⌐	
				⌐⌐	
				⌐⌐	
				⌐⌐	
				⌐⌐	
				⌐⌐	

DATE	FROM	EVENT/OCCASION	GIFT/GESTURE	THANK-YOU NOTE FINISHED	DATE SENT
				☐	
				☐	
				☐	
				☐	
				☐	
				☐	
				☐	
				☐	
				☐	

DATE	FROM	EVENT/OCCASION	GIFT/GESTURE	THANK-YOU NOTE FINISHED	DATE SENT
				☐	
				☐	
				☐	
				☐	
				☐	
				☐	
				☐	
				☐	
				☐	

DATE	FROM	EVENT/OCCASION	GIFT/GESTURE	THANK-YOU NOTE FINISHED	DATE SENT
				⌐⌐	
				⌐⌐	
				⌐⌐	
				⌐⌐	
				⌐⌐	
				⌐⌐	
				⌐⌐	
				⌐⌐	
				⌐⌐	

DATE	FROM	EVENT/OCCASION	GIFT/GESTURE	THANK-YOU NOTE FINISHED	DATE SENT
				⌞ ⌝	
				⌞ ⌝	
				⌞ ⌝	
				⌞ ⌝	
				⌞ ⌝	
				⌞ ⌝	
				⌞ ⌝	
				⌞ ⌝	
				⌞ ⌝	

DATE	FROM	EVENT/OCCASION	GIFT/GESTURE	THANK-YOU NOTE FINISHED	DATE SENT
				☐	
				☐	
				☐	
				☐	
				☐	
				☐	
				☐	
				☐	
				☐	

DATE	FROM	EVENT/OCCASION	GIFT/GESTURE	THANK-YOU NOTE FINISHED	DATE SENT
				☐	
				☐	
				☐	
				☐	
				☐	
				☐	
				☐	
				☐	
				☐	

DATE	FROM	EVENT/OCCASION	GIFT/GESTURE	THANK-YOU NOTE FINISHED	DATE SENT
				⌞⌝	
				⌞⌝	
				⌞⌝	
				⌞⌝	
				⌞⌝	
				⌞⌝	
				⌞⌝	
				⌞⌝	
				⌞⌝	

DATE	FROM	EVENT/OCCASION	GIFT/GESTURE	THANK-YOU NOTE FINISHED	DATE SENT
				☐	
				☐	
				☐	
				☐	
				☐	
				☐	
				☐	
				☐	

DATE	FROM	EVENT/OCCASION	GIFT/GESTURE	THANK-YOU NOTE FINISHED	DATE SENT
				☐	
				☐	
				☐	
				☐	
				☐	
				☐	
				☐	
				☐	
				☐	

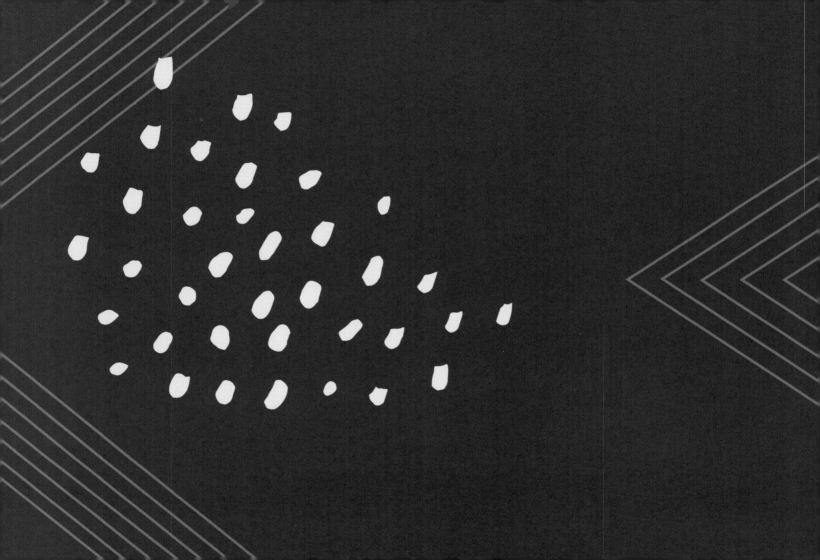

DATE	FROM	EVENT/OCCASION	GIFT/GESTURE	THANK-YOU NOTE FINISHED	DATE SENT
				⌐ ¬ ⌊ ⌋	
				⌐ ¬ ⌊ ⌋	
				⌐ ¬ ⌊ ⌋	
				⌐ ¬ ⌊ ⌋	
				⌐ ¬ ⌊ ⌋	
				⌐ ¬ ⌊ ⌋	
				⌐ ¬ ⌊ ⌋	
				⌐ ¬ ⌊ ⌋	
				⌐ ¬ ⌊ ⌋	

DATE	FROM	EVENT/OCCASION	GIFT/GESTURE	THANK-YOU NOTE FINISHED	DATE SENT
				☐	
				☐	
				☐	
				☐	
				☐	
				☐	
				☐	
				☐	
				☐	

DATE	FROM	EVENT/OCCASION	GIFT/GESTURE	THANK-YOU NOTE FINISHED	DATE SENT
				☐	
				☐	
				☐	
				☐	
				☐	
				☐	
				☐	
				☐	
				☐	

DATE	FROM	EVENT/OCCASION	GIFT/GESTURE	THANK-YOU NOTE FINISHED	DATE SENT
				☐	
				☐	
				☐	
				☐	
				☐	
				☐	
				☐	
				☐	
				☐	

DATE	FROM	EVENT/OCCASION	GIFT/GESTURE	THANK-YOU NOTE FINISHED	DATE SENT
				☐	
				☐	
				☐	
				☐	
				☐	
				☐	
				☐	
				☐	
				☐	

DATE	FROM	EVENT/OCCASION	GIFT/GESTURE	THANK-YOU NOTE FINISHED	DATE SENT
				☐	
				☐	
				☐	
				☐	
				☐	
				☐	
				☐	
				☐	
				☐	

DATE	FROM	EVENT/OCCASION	GIFT/GESTURE	THANK-YOU NOTE FINISHED	DATE SENT
				☐	
				☐	
				☐	
				☐	
				☐	
				☐	
				☐	
				☐	
				☐	

DATE	FROM	EVENT/OCCASION	GIFT/GESTURE	THANK-YOU NOTE FINISHED	DATE SENT
				⬜	
				⬜	
				⬜	
				⬜	
				⬜	
				⬜	
				⬜	
				⬜	
				⬜	

DATE	FROM	EVENT/OCCASION	GIFT/GESTURE	THANK-YOU NOTE FINISHED	DATE SENT
				☐	
				☐	
				☐	
				☐	
				☐	
				☐	
				☐	
				☐	
				☐	

DATE	FROM	EVENT/OCCASION	GIFT/GESTURE	THANK-YOU NOTE FINISHED	DATE SENT
				☐	
				☐	
				☐	
				☐	
				☐	
				☐	
				☐	
				☐	
				☐	

DATE	FROM	EVENT/OCCASION	GIFT/GESTURE	THANK-YOU NOTE FINISHED	DATE SENT
				☐	
				☐	
				☐	
				☐	
				☐	
				☐	
				☐	
				☐	
				☐	

DATE	FROM	EVENT/OCCASION	GIFT/GESTURE	THANK-YOU NOTE FINISHED	DATE SENT
				☐	
				☐	
				☐	
				☐	
				☐	
				☐	
				☐	
				☐	
				☐	

DATE	FROM	EVENT/OCCASION	GIFT/GESTURE	THANK-YOU NOTE FINISHED	DATE SENT
				☐	
				☐	
				☐	
				☐	
				☐	
				☐	
				☐	
				☐	

DATE	FROM	EVENT/OCCASION	GIFT/GESTURE	THANK-YOU NOTE FINISHED	DATE SENT
				⸢ ⸣	
				⸢ ⸣	
				⸢ ⸣	
				⸢ ⸣	
				⸢ ⸣	
				⸢ ⸣	
				⸢ ⸣	
				⸢ ⸣	
				⸢ ⸣	

DATE	FROM	EVENT/OCCASION	GIFT/GESTURE	THANK-YOU NOTE FINISHED	DATE SENT
				☐	
				☐	
				☐	
				☐	
				☐	
				☐	
				☐	
				☐	
				☐	

DATE	FROM	EVENT/OCCASION	GIFT/GESTURE	THANK-YOU NOTE FINISHED	DATE SENT
				⬜	
				⬜	
				⬜	
				⬜	
				⬜	
				⬜	
				⬜	
				⬜	
				⬜	

DATE	FROM	EVENT/OCCASION	GIFT/GESTURE	THANK-YOU NOTE FINISHED	DATE SENT
				☐	
				☐	
				☐	
				☐	
				☐	
				☐	
				☐	
				☐	
				☐	

DATE	FROM	EVENT/OCCASION	GIFT/GESTURE	THANK-YOU NOTE FINISHED	DATE SENT
				☐	
				☐	
				☐	
				☐	
				☐	
				☐	
				☐	
				☐	
				☐	

DATE	FROM	EVENT/OCCASION	GIFT/GESTURE	THANK-YOU NOTE FINISHED	DATE SENT
				☐	
				☐	
				☐	
				☐	
				☐	
				☐	
				☐	
				☐	
				☐	

DATE	FROM	EVENT/OCCASION	GIFT/GESTURE	THANK-YOU NOTE FINISHED	DATE SENT
				⬚	
				⬚	
				⬚	
				⬚	
				⬚	
				⬚	
				⬚	
				⬚	
				⬚	

DATE	FROM	EVENT/OCCASION	GIFT/GESTURE	THANK-YOU NOTE FINISHED	DATE SENT
				☐	
				☐	
				☐	
				☐	
				☐	
				☐	
				☐	
				☐	
				☐	

DATE	FROM	EVENT/OCCASION	GIFT/GESTURE	THANK-YOU NOTE FINISHED	DATE SENT
				☐	
				☐	
				☐	
				☐	
				☐	
				☐	
				☐	
				☐	
				☐	

DATE	FROM	EVENT/OCCASION	GIFT/GESTURE	THANK-YOU NOTE FINISHED	DATE SENT
				☐	
				☐	
				☐	
				☐	
				☐	
				☐	
				☐	
				☐	
				☐	

DATE	FROM	EVENT/OCCASION	GIFT/GESTURE	THANK-YOU NOTE FINISHED	DATE SENT
				☐	
				☐	
				☐	
				☐	
				☐	
				☐	
				☐	
				☐	
				☐	

DATE	FROM	EVENT/OCCASION	GIFT/GESTURE	THANK-YOU NOTE FINISHED	DATE SENT
				☐	
				☐	
				☐	
				☐	
				☐	
				☐	
				☐	
				☐	
				☐	

DATE	FROM	EVENT/OCCASION	GIFT/GESTURE	THANK-YOU NOTE FINISHED	DATE SENT
				☐	
				☐	
				☐	
				☐	
				☐	
				☐	
				☐	
				☐	
				☐	

DATE	FROM	EVENT/OCCASION	GIFT/GESTURE	THANK-YOU NOTE FINISHED	DATE SENT
				☐	
				☐	
				☐	
				☐	
				☐	
				☐	
				☐	
				☐	
				☐	

DATE	FROM	EVENT/OCCASION	GIFT/GESTURE	THANK-YOU NOTE FINISHED	DATE SENT
				☐	
				☐	
				☐	
				☐	
				☐	
				☐	
				☐	
				☐	
				☐	

DATE	FROM	EVENT/OCCASION	GIFT/GESTURE	THANK-YOU NOTE FINISHED	DATE SENT
				☐	
				☐	
				☐	
				☐	
				☐	
				☐	
				☐	
				☐	
				☐	

DATE	FROM	EVENT/OCCASION	GIFT/GESTURE	THANK-YOU NOTE FINISHED	DATE SENT
				☐	
				☐	
				☐	
				☐	
				☐	
				☐	
				☐	
				☐	
				☐	

DATE	FROM	EVENT/OCCASION	GIFT/GESTURE	THANK-YOU NOTE FINISHED	DATE SENT
				☐	
				☐	
				☐	
				☐	
				☐	
				☐	
				☐	
				☐	
				☐	

DATE	FROM	EVENT/OCCASION	GIFT/GESTURE	THANK-YOU NOTE FINISHED	DATE SENT
				☐	
				☐	
				☐	
				☐	
				☐	
				☐	
				☐	
				☐	
				☐	

DATE	FROM	EVENT/OCCASION	GIFT/GESTURE	THANK-YOU NOTE FINISHED	DATE SENT
				☐	
				☐	
				☐	
				☐	
				☐	
				☐	
				☐	
				☐	
				☐	

DATE	FROM	EVENT/OCCASION	GIFT/GESTURE	THANK-YOU NOTE FINISHED	DATE SENT
				☐	
				☐	
				☐	
				☐	
				☐	
				☐	
				☐	
				☐	
				☐	

DATE	FROM	EVENT/OCCASION	GIFT/GESTURE	THANK-YOU NOTE FINISHED	DATE SENT
				☐	
				☐	
				☐	
				☐	
				☐	
				☐	
				☐	
				☐	
				☐	

DATE	FROM	EVENT/OCCASION	GIFT/GESTURE	THANK-YOU NOTE FINISHED	DATE SENT
				☐	
				☐	
				☐	
				☐	
				☐	
				☐	
				☐	
				☐	
				☐	

DATE	FROM	EVENT/OCCASION	GIFT/GESTURE	THANK-YOU NOTE FINISHED	DATE SENT
				☐	
				☐	
				☐	
				☐	
				☐	
				☐	
				☐	
				☐	
				☐	

DATE	FROM	EVENT/OCCASION	GIFT/GESTURE	THANK-YOU NOTE FINISHED	DATE SENT
				☐	
				☐	
				☐	
				☐	
				☐	
				☐	
				☐	
				☐	
				☐	

DATE	FROM	EVENT/OCCASION	GIFT/GESTURE	THANK-YOU NOTE FINISHED	DATE SENT
				⬜	
				⬜	
				⬜	
				⬜	
				⬜	
				⬜	
				⬜	
				⬜	
				⬜	

DATE	FROM	EVENT/OCCASION	GIFT/GESTURE	THANK-YOU NOTE FINISHED	DATE SENT
				☐	
				☐	
				☐	
				☐	
				☐	
				☐	
				☐	
				☐	
				☐	

DATE	FROM	EVENT/OCCASION	GIFT/GESTURE	THANK-YOU NOTE FINISHED	DATE SENT
				☐	
				☐	
				☐	
				☐	
				☐	
				☐	
				☐	
				☐	
				☐	

DATE	FROM	EVENT/OCCASION	GIFT/GESTURE	THANK-YOU NOTE FINISHED	DATE SENT
				☐	
				☐	
				☐	
				☐	
				☐	
				☐	
				☐	
				☐	
				☐	